Natalie
the
Narwhal

Kelsey Sweetland
Author and Illustrator

My Dream For the Ocean

My love for the ocean began when I was three years old. I fell in love with the documentary *Blue Planet*. I learned about ocean ecosystems, coral reefs, and how in even the deepest depths of the ocean, there is life. Since then, my love of the ocean has grown into a fighting passion to protect its majestic creatures.

As I learned more about the ocean, I realized that many people do not know the damage caused by commercial fishing, pollution, and oil spills. The ocean is not an inexhaustible supply of food or a convenient dumping ground. It can be permanently damaged and right now we have the chance to make change. As Dr. Sylvia Earle says, "The next five years may be the most important in the next ten thousand for our planet."

When I heard Sylvia Earle's TED Talk I learned that 90% of the big fish in the ocean are gone due to overfishing, I realized that some people don't even know that they are eating endangered fish! For example, the orange roughy is a 100+ year old fish but we are pulling them out of the ocean faster than they can reach maturity and lay eggs.

One highly destructive part of commercial fishing is the use of trawlers, nets, and longlines. I urge you to research each of these fishing practices for they are destroying our ocean. (Oceana's Bycatch Report is an excellent source.) Trawlers scrape the ocean floor, destroying coral, and it's estimated by PETA that for every pound of fish, 20 pounds of "bycatch" is killed–seals, dolphins, turtles and whales.

But not all hope is lost. The world has many nonprofits working to help our oceans by removing trash and protecting coral reefs. But even then, we need more people to realize that the ocean is in danger. If this intimidates you, start small. One simple idea is to use Monterey Bay Aquarium's Seafood Watch app to see which fish are safe to eat. Start asking seafood restaurants if they have line-caught (single hook, not "longline") sustainable fish options on their menu.

Remember, it starts with the people. And look at me–I love the ocean, so I wrote a book to spread the word. It does not matter how old or young you are. Because right now you are reading the work of a 13 year old, and hopefully I have changed your mind.

MISSION **BLUE**™
SYLVIA EARLE ALLIANCE

By purchasing Natalie the Narwhal, you will be protecting oceans and marine life all around the world!

My dream for this book is to have children and parents grow a deeper affinity for the ocean and marine life. I am donating a portion of my profits to Mission Blue, a non-profit organization working to create a worldwide network of marine protected areas. Your purchase helps protect our endangered oceans.

Dedication

I dedicate this book to my family and
Mission Blue

In sun, snow and rain Natalie would be found carving the glittering ice blocks on the surface of the ocean.

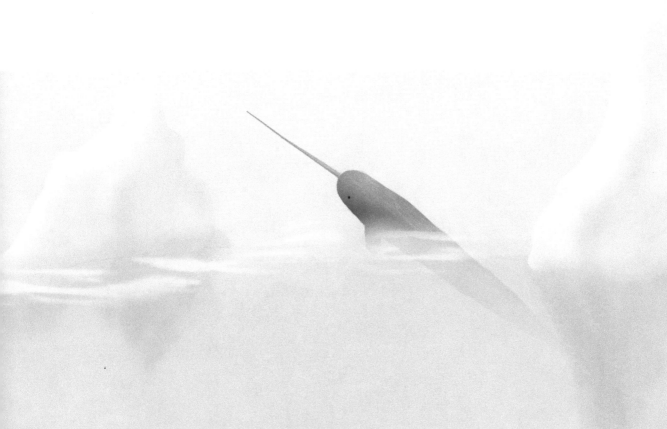

Natalie loved to wake up with light bouncing off her ice sculptures, making the rainbows dance around her room. Usually the light woke her up like an alarm clock and sent her off to work, but today Natalie's parents woke up first.

The moment she peeked out of her room she knew another peptalk from her parents was coming. Natalie did not like their peptalks.

As she often did, Natalie
thought back to a painful memory
from many years ago...

It had all started one frosty
morning when Natalie's parents were
creating an undersea home for their town
mayor and dragged her along.

But halfway through the tour, Natalie had
gotten bored.

She slipped away, grabbed a block of ice
to carve, and pulled the ice down into the
fridgid waters below.

Next she found a giant rock and set it on the ice to pin it to the ocean floor.

The ice suddenly skidded from under the rock and crashed into the mayor's house!

Her parents darted out, looked at the wreckage and back to the ice floating upwards.

Natalie saw that they were spitting bubbles from their blowholes.

Uh oh, she thought. And she dashed home.

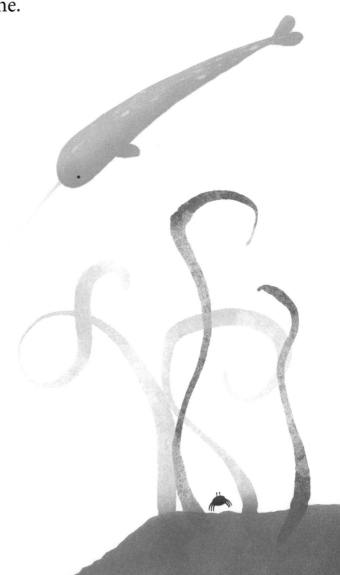

"Natalie!" her mom sang, snapping
Natalie out of her memory. Today Natalie
knew that she could no longer avoid
going to work with her parents.
But if she went with them,
she might wreck
everything just
like that day
many
years
ago.

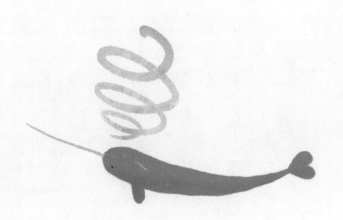

She crawled out of her bedroom and her dad said,
"Today is the day, Natalie!"
Natalie lowered her head.
"I know. I'll come with you to your new building."
"You'll be fine," her dad said. "I am sure you won't wreck anything this time!"
Natalie's heart told her otherwise.

Natalie watched hesitantly as her family showed her the finished house.

"We completed the building right in time for the North Sea Grand Opening!" they proudly sang.

Suddenly, a mighty current blew through the building...

… and giant iceburgs started knocking off rocks and debris from the house! Everyone swam for cover in a small cave.

When the storm had stopped its whirling and churning, the building was peppered with holes and craters.

To complete the disaster, the roof had fully toppled away.

Natalie's parents hung their heads and looked in dismay at their wrecked building.

Natalie felt bad for her parents, so she swam home and thought of a plan.

Natalie had been searching for a way to make up for the Mayor's building she had destroyed so long ago. So after everyone was asleep, she slipped out to fix her parent's house as a surprise.

When Natalie got to the broken house, no matter how hard she tried, she could not find the right size rocks to patch up the endless holes.

By midnight she began to lose hope.

As she dragged herself back home, she
happened upon a wise
old jellyfish.

He asked Natalie where she was headed. She explained that she had tried to finish the building that her parents made, but she just couldn't do it. He tapped a tentacle to his squishy head and said,

"What is your talent? Find that, and you will be able to solve whatever problem life throws at you."

And with that, he swam away.

His words
got Natalie
thinking...What if
she could use ice
to patch up the
holes? She could
be done by
morning!
So she
excitedly set off
to the ocean's
surface.

Natalie used her ice carving skills to fill
the damage caused by the storm.

After the sun was near the horizon,
Natalie's building was finished.

She swam home tired but pleased with herself and announced
the good news. Her parents were so happy they tapped horns
and shimmied with joy!
Her mom exclaimed that
she would immediately
tell the mayor
about Natalie's
achievement.

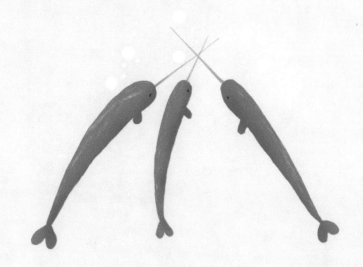

The next day the mayor called for a party in celebration of Natalie the Narwhal!

The whole town gurgled with excitement and the mayor called for attention. "Not only are we celebrating the recovery of one of our newest buildings, but we might have a new designer on our construction team."

The crowd bubbled excitedly, and the mayor said,
"Natalie, will you be one of our builders, *and* our first professional ice carver?"

Natalie exclaimed,
"Yes!"

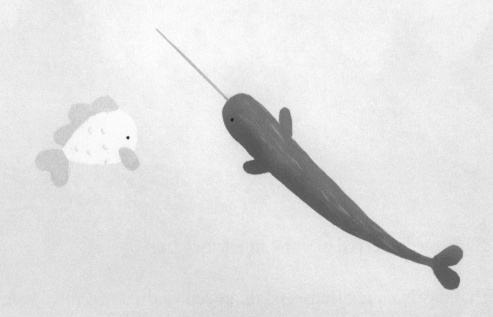

The crowd cheered and the music began.

That day Natalie discovered that even in the most murky circumstances your gifts can help you shine.

About Me

I am Kelsey Sweetland, 13 years old, and l live with my mom, dad, brother, and bengal cat in Los Gatos, California. My favorite pastimes are to draw, paint, read, and play with my brother. Over the 2020 summer I spent my time creating Natalie the Narwhal and became a junior PADI certified scuba diver!

My motivation to write this book started with a trip to the Island School in the Bahamas. I tracked sea turtles, worked on an aquaponics farm, and learned the basics of ocean sustainability.

When I was snorkeling above a hammerhead shark and then held a young sea turtle in my lap, I felt protective and passionate not just for this turtle–but for all turtles and marine life around the world.

When I returned home, I decided that I will not stand by while my ocean transforms into a garbage dump, has more plastic than fish in the sea, and ocean acidification crumbles coral reefs into bones.

My mission is just beginning. I am driven to inspire others to stand up as I do. We need to tell our leaders that we want an ocean filled with life and beauty.

I am now reaching an age where I have a voice in my community. But I do not just have any voice. I am a voice with a mission.

Follow me on my Instagram page KelseySweetlandPublishing where I post my artwork, facts about the environment, and promote my books!

KELSEYSWEETLANDPUBLISHING

Gratitude

Thank you...

To Hillbrook School and the Scott Center for Social Entrepreneurship for inspiring me to make an impact in the world.

To the Bahamas Island School for showing me ways to live everyday life without harming the environment.

To Young Inklings for their mentorship and support.

To ocean activist, Sylvia Earle, for her TED Talk and inspiration. I now share your wish for the ocean and will do all I can to help.

And last but not least, I thank my family for supporting my dreams, being there for me, and reminding me that nothing is impossible.

Printed in the USA
CPSIA information can be obtained
at www.ICGtesting.com
LVHW071021091123
763115LV00063B/989